SCARING THE BEARS

Whether prayerful or analytical, full of joy or touched with terror, the voice of this poet always gives us what the best poetry delivers: a richness in its textures and a close attention to the kind of concrete details of life that, in the words of Flannery O'Connor, "make actual the mystery of our position on earth." This is a strong collection, long anticipated and a pleasure to have in hand.

—Judson Mitcham, Georgia Poet Laureate (2012–2019)
and author of *A Little Salvation*, *This April Day*,
and *Somewhere in Ecclesiastes*

The church house and home life are not far off in Gordon Johnston's poems, and the words of the prophets are timbre to his thought. Emotion ties the poet to the family. Parents and kids make their pronounced appearances, whether before a final departure or in the daily life of the family. Johnston reminds us that it is not a failure of art or of the imagination to love the world.

—Kevin Cantwell, author of *One of Those Russian Novels*
and *Something Black in the Green Part of Your Eye*

MERCER
UNIVERSITY

MERCER UNIVERSITY PRESS

Endowed by

TOM WATSON BROWN
and
THE WATSON-BROWN FOUNDATION, INC.

SCARING THE BEARS

Poems

Gordon Johnston

MERCER UNIVERSITY PRESS
Macon, Georgia
2021

MUP/ P619

Published by Mercer University Press
1501 Mercer University Drive
Macon, Georgia 31207

25 24 23 22 21 5 4 3 2 1

Books published by Mercer University Press are printed on acid-free paper that meets the requirements of the American National Standard for Information Sciences—Permanence of Paper for Printed Library Materials.

Printed and bound in the United States.

This book is set in Adobe Garamond Pro.

Cover/jacket design by Burt&Burt.

Library of Congress Cataloging-in-Publication Data

Names: Johnston, Gordon, 1967- author.
Title: Scaring the bears : poems / Gordon Johnston.
Description: Macon, Georgia : Mercer University Press, 2021. |
Identifiers: LCCN 2020050712 | ISBN 9780881467796 (paperback)
Subjects: LCGFT: Poetry.
Classification: LCC PS3610.O386 S28 2021 | DDC 811/.6--dc23
LC record available at https://lccn.loc.gov/2020050712

For Pam

“Practice resurrection.”
—Wendell Berry
“Manifesto: The Mad Farmer
Liberation Front”

CONTENTS

ACKNOWLEDGMENTS

The author thanks the editors of the following journals, books, and anthologies where earlier versions of the following poems in this collection first appeared:

Southern Poetry Review: "Durable Goods," "Sweep," "Ash Monday," "Men's Fashions at 40"

Writing on Napkins at the Sunshine Club: "Ties," "Her Father's Pants"

Gravity's Light Grip (chapbook, Perkolator Press): "Ties"

The Southern Poetry Anthology, Volume 5: Georgia: "Bear," "Crutches"

Atlanta Review and the anthology *The Gift of Experience*: "Wedding Ring Found on Adams Street, Spring Friday"

Denver Quarterly: "Bird Calendar"

Stone, River, Sky: An Anthology of Georgia Poets: "Canoe"

Ocmulgee National Monument: A Brief History with Field Notes: "Bridge Swallow," "Blackberries"

Phi Kapp Phi Forum: "Attention Deficit Disorder"

While writing the poems in this collection, I received moral, spiritual, and material support from more sources than I can name. I am abidingly grateful for that community. I offer special thanks to my partner Pamela and my three children for their patient, supportive, hilarious spirits and for keeping our home so quiet mornings. These poems took on greater grace and clarity thanks to the suggestions of Bill King, Judson Mitcham, Kevin Cantwell, Anya Krugovoy Silver, Michael Cass, Van Henderson, Margaret Harrington, and Sarah Hughes. John Prine, the Wood Brothers, Mavis Staples, and Wilco floated me out of some deep doubts. Sherrie Jamison's art and Roger Jamison's anagama kiln have helped me keep the faith by giving me a place in a congregation of craftspeople. Matt Harper writes with me Fridays. Marc Jolley at Mercer University Press kept asking. I'm also grateful for the financial support of the Faculty Research and Writing Colloquium at Mercer University and for Griffith funds for travel from Mercer's English Department. Writing residencies at the Hambidge Center for the Creative Arts and Sciences and the Lillian Smith Center gave me the stretches of uninterrupted time to revise necessary for the book to mature.

Things of Earth

Bear

From the deep shade under the laurel an air
    a breath the blurred beam of animal vision
        lands on him, a man of forty in worn-out woods

He turns his head and each sees and scents
    the other in a second that has no center,
        that is focused and eternal and over

The oldest paths in their bodies open and he
    is anciently human in his loafers and sweat
        which strangle her their smell like the taste

of brass crowding all she knows out of her warm
    bear brain so that she rises huffing from rooting
        the grubs out of the rotted log and because he

stops because he freezes as he sees her the way a threat
    to a cub would freeze she drops again goes into motion
        What he thinks is not that ten years have passed since he

has walked in the woods not that she smells like his ex-wife's
    schnauzer not even that he will die now what he thinks is PBS
        a televised ranger saying *Bluff charge* and *You shouldn't run* and

he doesn't but he has flinched and she is upslope of him a little
    she is already there and by the time the TV of memory says *Fall*
        and he does she is striking him snout-first knocking him backwards

his palms grazing her jowl fur in a touch that in slo-mo would be tender
    and he smells the loam along her muzzle loam of hunger so that
        that smell is what he curls around fetal on the gravel path born

again his glands open his body perceiving that there is nothing to save
as her teeth touch together through the tail of his shirt her breath
on his lower back the nose dry and moving exactly like a dog's

blowing at his neck his forehead where it meets his knees his shoes
which he doesn't know are saving him because yesterday he had them
polished and the tang in them is like a blunt blow between her eyes

He feels her weight gone from the ground around him
his eyes open in the circle he has made of himself
and already he loves her who has let him live.

The Things of Earth

Some Sunday nights we sang the whole service,
people raising their hands for the oldest hymns.
It was my kind of church—just the piano, a dozen
grown-ups and half as many kids, the preacher
letting us sit through every song. We casted down
our golden crowns around the glassy sea.
If you tried, you could hear any one voice
except Mr. Peavey, who sang the words
more inside his mouth than out. These nights,
I didn't pester my mother for gum or twist
Wrigley's wrappers into little silver cups,
only listened to the weird words saved up for Sunday:
burden, thou, diadem, thee. We sang *The things
of earth will grow strangely dim* and I saw twilight
out the open windows on the long grass all the way
to the road. Preacher Cliatt, fingertips tented,
head bowed, asked some deacon *Close us in prayer,*
though Miss Rose's and Brother Bill Elliot's hands
still reached for certain songs.
                                                  Rare nights when you could
ask and then receive just exactly what you wanted,
it seemed to me all should stay until every hand was answered.
You should know it's not yours to close, not the night
or God's ears or hands or the mouths of people
asking for something that in the singing everybody else
finds they wanted, too. I didn't hear *prayer* so much as
close us in. I wanted to stay out, singing with Miss Rose
I come to the garden alone—all she ever asked for,
and what we should have sung with her, alone in unison,
until she got ready herself to go out in the dark.

Ties

Sundays only I woke early enough to see
my father cinch them up into the gable of his collar.
He misjudged often, especially if I was talking to him:
when he knew he was off, he seized the knot, two fingers
over it, two around it, and yanked the silk down hard.
Ties: a man's secret handshake with himself—
a strange, heraldic hank of ceremony, fatherliness, mastery.
Useless, utterly necessary, they were a double lock against
some dread laxity, all order and propriety were pressed
in their odd folds.

You could play nothing with them—not snake or highway
or Indian headband. Their texture, their taper, these killed it.
They were bought by women, worn by men. Ladies hovered
over racks of them in stores, draping three or four over
cellophaned shirts and against the sleeves of coats
lined with hidden pockets.

My father never entirely submitted. He tore his off
before we left the church parking lot. Never walked in
from work but with tie wrenched down, top button sprung.

A boy of a certain age could no longer wear the clip-on kind
with honor, and so I stood beside my father, repeating
his motions in the mirror. My knots never took.
An engineer, no patient teacher where symmetry mattered,
my father always took my tie himself, talking me through
his ancient noosing. Once, he stood behind me:
I watched my father's arms knot silk onto me. It was summer.
He had switched to short sleeves. His veiny hands close,
busy, out of place over my heart. I couldn't follow his fingers.

I think he gave up, then. *Keep one knotted,* he said.
A solid color goes with anything.

On my bus, a dark-eyed senior girl turned and looked softly
down at me. She said my sister had told her I couldn't tie a tie.
She put a folded paper in my hand.
At home I locked my door, opened her letter.
1. Let the slender end hang to where a woman's breast
would be.
I don't remember two.
She brought me, first try, to a perfect Windsor.
I tied and retied seven times, thinking with each pass,
where a woman's breast would be, imagining, of course,
her breast, offered quiet for my initiation.
I stood at the mirror, ghosts of her small hands about me,
waiting to show him this new knot at my throat.

My Freshman Year Flannel

is as old as Jesus. Bought off clearance a whole
half-life ago, she hasn't faded. When I shrug her
onto my shoulders every third October, I remember.
Today I have just ridden my scooter home in the rain,
each drop a small nail of resurrecting pain, until,
chinos soaked, my bared arms and chest a relief map
of chilblain, this old, soft skin takes me in.
She has lost her cool. She is '80s oversized, a muted
navy, green, and gold in shades that three decades ago
looked old. Like me, *vintage* vintage, she has grown into
what she pretended to be. She swaddles my cold body
in my leaving of home, my first living alone in Rome,
Georgia, when my life fit in a Honda hatchback.
I sit and thaw. Blood returns to my toes. The shirt warms.
I should rise. Instead, I write this in my freshman form.

Dropping My Son off at School

"Message in a Bottle" plays in my truck's tape deck —
his choice. *Love can mend your life or love can break your heart.*
At fourteen, sure I had learned this truth already, I sang along,
savoring the words and the hard guitar, as jaded and jagged as me,
so I'm sad and pleased he likes it, too -- this throwback linearity,
FF and PROG, of his father's analog adolescence. I imagine
the capstans spooling patience from me to him, then back again.
I want to say he's not just a castaway.
                                                  Quiet, un-sullen, once-shaven,
to be freed from braces in two days, less and less a boy each dawn
in a growth I pray goes on, he rides, gripped by a bassline, a flanger,
as I was. (Am.) The thin brown ribbon—worn out, really—rolls on.
What will he be? *Not alone at being alone*, the young Sting sings—
the line that kept me secret company. I rewind to finding my fidelity,
to learning my own lyric through the wow and flutter. He opens
his door. *Later, Dad*, he says. I feel like his little brother.

Crutches

In high school, I loved every girl who had them—fell for little fingers
curled around the foam rubber grips, for the chunky plaster cast full

as a dance card with names, for the bent-knee peep-show of toes
glossed Candy Apple, nails a row of shrinking red faces like those

secretly hollow dolls that nest inside each other. Karen Wynn fringed
the cut-off left leg of her Levis, teasing the threads fine as mohair 'til

they tickled my dreams. She swung between them from Chorus to
Chemistry, ticking *crutch-tip, toe, crutch-tip, toe*, my heart knocking

to her slow rhythm. Their casts were public as our paint rock, where
at night pairs of us sprayed names and loves in big, first-grade letters.

A hurt girl's homeroom would kneel one at a time and scribble: in-
side, her fibula in the warm grip of girl muscle knit. All I knew to

write was my crooked name, nowhere near her toes, but in the middle,
where the snow of plaster was deepest, where, itching under my gray

lead cursive, she might lay her hand.

Analog

We'll start with a dog meeting a dog—
not snout-to-snout but nose to tail—
and how my human version has always
been sniffing some other stray's music:
the unzip or unclip of the vinyl tape case
on the seat of someone's Maverick or Monza
so that the bands and albums slotted there
like the lines of this poem could be read
like a signature scent—a balance of recog-
nition and strangeness (records I loved
laddered in with music I wished to meet)—
that held the promise of a two-mutt pack.
The Who. The Time. DMC and ELO.
To hunt together, teen lobos need known range
that holds new places to go. The key turned
(ACC), plastic case clicked open like a book,
cassette pinched and extracted and fed
into the deck as its cover drops like a rocket stage—
all of this done with one expert hand—
my ears prick for a new howl to home in on
and answer across the wild, lonesome land.

Attention Deficit Disorder

Where, O God, did this boy bust the budget—
searching every dirt road's shoulder for arrowheads,
eye-gleaning the grader's pile for flint with crescent edges,

mapping Mirkwood in Math for Daily Living?
I used to notch the blade-sight of my Daisy's barrel
letter by letter along a pop can's cursive and gut-shoot

every *O*. Where did that steady aimed-ness go?
Bible drills reamed it out, maybe, or lines learned for plays
maxed out my memory. Women, once I woke to them,

wore me out. The timbre of girls talking brimmed me over—
their ripple and breath, the way they laughed. All summer
they didn't sweat. Their other world in this one still makes me

straddle both. I lean too far this way, then that.
The old man I hope to be finds, bakes, and antler-knaps
keen flakes from chunks of chert. He gets paid to zero-in

hunters' guns (three shots through the same hole says *Done*).
Calm as a water clock, he's learned what to overlook.
The girls he whirls, Texas-two-stepping 'round

the honky tonk, feel his secret stillness. To be
the centered spindle on which they turn—!
Father, make me him. Give me attention to burn.

Men's Fashions at Forty

On you, everything is vintage—
the new jeans, dyed in diesel oil
and the dapper shoes with soles
uncomfortably thin. All the old skins—

the freshman year flannel, lax and warm,
your father's bachelor houndstooth coat
(borrowed, never returned), the sneakers
bought to walk your wife through labor—

wear like ironic grins. In the mirror,
you're not retro, but has-been.
Who wants to be haberdashed with history?
Your choices, like your hair, have thinned.

Clothes don't make the man,
yet everything drapes like—what?
Raiment? Is that a monk's habit?
(Are you older than Merton yet?)

At thirty, your father's cufflinks,
Like the silk-backed vest you wore
to the Costello concert, were a way
to put on age without wisdom.

Now, you know what you know.
Your boho goatee, greyed, is hobo.
This tux has outlasted the marriage
you bought it to best-man in.

Tell yourself you knew those two
had always refused to admit impediments.

Shrug into its black, silky heft: trim
in the shoulders, tight across the chest.

Eleven funerals the last four years:
For those, no question how to dress.
(Your vasectomy felt like a twelfth—
a bag of frozen peas as a compress.)

For twenty years she has put on the knowledge
of you: new wine in your same old skins.
They spun off sons, those little deaths.
Is not the body more than clothes? Yes.

Then why are you holding your breath?

Material:

(1) Cloth my mother bought by the yard,
cut into shapes using patterns thin as Bible pages,
then ran through her Singer, her fingers framing
a plunging needle. The halo of light hid her face.
Dresses for my sisters came of it and, once, a red
chambray shirt—beautiful, simple, itchy
except at its open collar, sewed only for me.
(2) An adjective I learned in college
when Dr. Wingard scribbled in red that my description
of my mother's father's farm was not material to
the meaning of *whinnying stable* in *Fern Hill.*
I meant Dylan Thomas was a man grown out
of a boy cut out of a farm that was almost his,
as I was and hadn't known before the poem read me
in a pool of light as my roommates slept.
My prof had a point: freshmen think they are
material to everything. (They are.)
(3) An adjective in an old Madonna song
for the one world worth living in—also for the girl
who sings it, the persona if you count the song
as a poem, which it isn't, though like *Fern Hill*
it wishes for freedom and substantiation through things—
the sabbath in the pebble of the holy stream, bling.
(4) My soul, subtracted from the subjects
that choose me, cut from my thin paper, like breath
subtracted from song. These words make a shape
I call mine. This pencil stitches out a solitude
that lets others almost enter—wear the red chambray
that my mother pieced, young. A song is not
a shirt, a pebble, a scribbled page. A song is not
material. A song is sung.

Roseola

After four days of fever and two more of rash, my boy,
almost two, has come through.

Growling, he brings a t-rex to this morning table, not to celebrate
but because he goes on.

Blond Buddha of the bunched-up diaper, he is back, busy, beautifully
empty, bearing extinction green, orange,

and brown through his mother's carnivorous kitchen.
The fork in the road is here, where I make him mean something,

milk the irony of a dinosaur
of imperishable plastic—twitch the line to show you the earth's

awful incisors. Instead, I will sit still.
Go where the mind of a father pushing forty goes. Love is

seeing what you have to lose
and losing the you that demands to know.

I sit. He plays. No poem. We are a nothing as brilliant as snow.

November

The last gift from my folks is a bag of green tomatoes
handed through my truck window before I pull out
from the home I was given to the one I try to give
my boys. *Put them in the sun*, my mother says,
though she knows I already know to. At home, I do.

They sit in a window, so round they seem about to roll
from the sill. Their skins shine like the inside of a lime.
The first frost glitters on the neighbor's roof behind them.
I see my father going vine to vine in the weather he has so
carefully minded, stealing hard fruit from the coming freeze.

Day by day, the heirlooms soften and orange up until,
come from work, I can see their color three shades richer
since I brewed the morning coffee—last red swell of summer
held, like my homes, in a light that ripens them.

Wedding Ring Found on Adams Street

All weekend they call, none of them new losers.
Left third finger long bare, each still chooses hope.
Some dial with that finger for luck, some cross it
As best they can over pinky or finger finger.
I say no to all of them: *No, this ring is plain—*
cheap electroplate worn silver around the rims.
No initials, date, or loving code letters its inner eternity.
With this ring, I thee wed, they all said, or something like it,
not counting on losing a symbol of love, loop, closure.
They tell me stories, describe what they can't replace,
hoping that I am a magnet for slipped symbols,
that diving for the foul ball or walking the dog
a glint from some grassy cranny will draw me,
that I will lift into light the precious zero that outgrew them.
Professor, doctor, neighbor, cop—all call looking
for a one-link chain.

I bought another one, this caller says, *'til my real one turns up.*
He can't give such a thing to himself. My father's father
made his own, filing from a steel nut morning after
morning threads and flat hexagonal faces until
what once had bolted together a boiler fastened flesh.
Cleave, we've all said—and do, at least to the symbol,
to what we thought we were getting into. A wholeness,
a predictable, charged curve like those toy race tracks
we played with as boys. The elegant girding of the digit
shows that what we have given the girl costs, cuts glass,
and glitters in churches.

I don't call these callers brother. I grit my teeth to hold in
what we all learn but can't say: that the moon in its changes
is a fitter emblem—the moon that fills and empties and has

less gravity, a dark side, scars, a man in it somewhere,
aloof and lost as a slipped balloon. I can't say this because they
need this circle, need something to live up to that goes on
even if they lose it—something that waits always to be found.

You Can Have It

I waited to hear it from my father as I held his Gibson six-string,
his pick between my lips—ached for his father to say it, too,
as his hand under mine stilled the barrel of his old rifle.
My finger curled in his around the steel crescent of trigger,
our one breath held, a corked skin of No. 9 oil and cordite.

In our high school library, the girl I liked to read with said it.
That night, we let her car radio play while each of us slipped
into the other, then came back out feeling alive and full grown
and more alone. The dash lit her face as she drove me home.

On a river at 20, I woke after it went unspoken by the rapid
that swallowed my boat and stole my left boot—though me she
spit out on the rocks still breathing, a flake of mica in my mouth.
Some nights, I'm sure I lie there still, wet and cold as birth.

Four days I knew and was (almost) known. I passed through.
Gibson, gun, Gail, and shoal have me still. Now I say it to you.

Hanging My Shirts

Morning

Fresh washed or just worn, as they drape the shoulder-slope
of the wire hanger, they have wrinkles. Hatched from the drier
the cotton is rucked and seam-puckered by a Sahara dervish,
so warm, one must be put on, as white against my skin as
new-baked bread against brown crust. Within this unbuttoned skin,
between dressed and undressed, alone, I wear candlelight.
Already deliciously, mortally cooling, the cloth begins to wick
from my chest, arms, and shoulder blades a second heat—
my own, which I try and fail to feel. I shuck it off, single-button it,
hook it in the closet. The small, glowing glory of raiment will wait
and wait for me—rumpled, arms open. A shape I can always be.

Evening

The other wrinkling is from wear—from my motion through
the used and easy air, from having sheltered a body from weather.
The yoke kinked by the hard rungs of a metal chair, sleeves
by the meetings of my day—soul in flesh in shirt in company
or in the car or by water reading or scribbling like this or washing
the coffee pot or pointing out to wife. brother, or child, the first
gloam star. All saved in this thinning linen. I can stand knowing
these creases will be rinsed away. The salt of shaken hands in my cuff,
the beer drop dried on my placket—they can't be kept. But often
I let them rest in my weft, these motes of human communion.
No flannel wants to be freed of second-hand perfume, that light,
leavening rose-ghost left by a cheek against a chest pocket,
so I hang it like a small censer for a while. Let it sweeten my room.

Durable Goods

Durable Goods

Demand for them is down, the commentator says—a bad sign.
People can't afford the pressed metal boxes that cool
their perishables and cleanse their delicates. I wait
for the number to call to ask this question: why is desire
not enough? For I have it in spades for preservation, cleansing,
agitation. A durable good is so far past due, my one man's
deprivation ought to give rise to a region-wide recovery.
The sail-less Maersk ships, bigger than malls, ferrying tonnages
of containers, should all be thrumming through the ocean to me
and my house, where need is so dire, so strong and centripetal
that it must make their compass needles read wrong, must draw
them to a pitiful new pole—a negation that the planet turns on.
No phone number, though. It isn't a call-in show. And why ask
when you already know. Desire is not demand—that enormous *we*
that will have its wish whatever it costs. Desire accepts—expects—
to be told *No*. Can prosper on it. Deferred, desire grows.
Demand refused explodes.

The problem is the keeping, not the having—good always *goes*.
Follow the needle tracks back until, one by one, they vanish:
the arm of your junkie niece is clean. You hold her again
as a baby. Or heft the hammer and square that framed
the home before this home. The hands skilled at using them
are gone. The blackened skillet and cornbread mold, the churn,
a hand-smithed clevis—durable ghosts gather as you grow older,
as you keep on keeping these things that gone souls own.
They hold their forms. Good is a right grip struck on such tools—
a certainty, a seasoned grasp of what mortal needs each can fill,
and how. Fire, nail, muscle, mule, made to do their lasting work—
the hammer's rhythm, the plowing pace, the flue hum—sacraments

that let generations hold their place in the world and their world
in its place, alive and in truck with mystery, singing one part
in a local, mortal harmony. This waiting is not better, though it opens
empty time in our lives for pictures and sugar, boxes to talk and play,
to make music for us. The ships come on, homing, full of their barren,
stillborn Christmas. They will until we demand a living that isn't debt.

Burning the Christmas Greens

Once the backyard sky teeters
between night and day—when there's
the least light left in which to lay wadded
newspaper in a ring of rocks or an iron bowl—
begin. Lop a branch from the tree's bottom—
only one—and bend it back on itself three times.
Green-break it, not in two. The limb will be a stiff coil
of barked rope. Lay this looped wood on the wads, then
light one. Watch the yellow blade stand up straight.
Once needles fizz and dried sap cracks, turn back
to the tree and choose whether to let it go whole,
a fast, epic flare, or branch by branch, as it grew.
Do it differently than you have done it before.
Lean in. Receive the heat on your hands as
the fir's last gift, unwrapping, years of sun
unscrolling. Breathe in the burning grain.
Hear the flame. The smoke will write
to the early stars in a quick, vertical
cursive. Catch all you can.
Be its lonely reader.

Bird Calendar

And on Saturday, February 5, I find him, in deep emerald profile—
the Yellow-Billed Oxpecker, whom, had I been Adam, I'd have named
the Lipstick Bird for his ruddy beak tip, or, better, Red-Eyed Ox Driver.
Driver, not *pecker*, because he's a high-headed bird, with a stern,
blood-sharp eye, a beak-tipper—by all appearances no prissy tweeter,
tick-picker though he is. *Eastern and Southern Africa, an obligate*
parasite, says Audubon. *It not only feeds but also courts a mate*
on the backs of water buffalo, antelope, and rhino. What a thing to find
this early in the morning, robins by the dozen hopping in red rubber
waistcoats outside my window, this early in the morning and on
someone's anniversary, too, on the day certain strangers will first kiss
then forever after tell it, how when lips met the earth threw a rod,
broke an axle, *some*thing, and from then on lurched along differently,
dromedary, with a sunny hide neither had seen before bearing them both
along like a muscular, threadbare carpet. And here I am, I *am*, saying it,
shameless: African cattle birds are to be envied. They are love itself,
dating behind the ears of elephants, feeding one another the minimal irks
of their animal county. How their hollow bones must fill with satisfaction
this one morning it will always be.

For the Wedding

This is another verse of the song your mother started singing
low and to herself, when she was all her own, under her breath,
so low it took your father to catch it. At first he didn't know he heard it,
though he was humming along before he knew he knew the tune

or maybe he knew right off, as my own father did: he saw a girl
in his landlord's wedding picture and hitchhiked from Clemson
to Charlotte with a record under his arm to meet her, bring her
some music. She had her own. One date and he hitched home.

While he walked the shoulder, the song got stronger. Softer.
Soon he bought another record and thumbed back.
Let me thank, now, the strangers who picked him up,
upon whose trusting whim I am contingent. Let me

thank my daddy's thumb, my mother's face for its flash-
caught, strangely certain smile. Let us all thank the song
that has sung us here, that we couldn't sing for ourselves.
Now a new song starts. Listen. Hum. Be ready to sing your part.

Thirty Five

Birth comes 'round again year after year and it's best
to rise early into it, to get up alone in the dark house,
deliver yourself between night and morning as the stars
fall asleep. The quiet will remind you you learned to talk
and it will teach you if you let it be. You don't have to go
out and look at the moon turning to a lozenge of milk
in the egg-blue air, but this bears knowing. Change
you can't see—a daily difference barely detectable—
merits awareness like getting up merits coffee, black
in the carafe, then caramel as it eddies up the inner cup,
ablend with the cream you already drizzled in so the coffee
in its pour stirs itself and the bitterness eases. Why is half
and half not whole? At thirty-five who has to ask?
You know now: halves are better. The five you alternately
are beat oneness. You are one-fifth of a half happy.
In two days, the government will give you an extra hour
of light each evening as a gift. It is your duty to waste it
and now is the time not to plan how. As the sun grows round,
caught fish and early attempts at heavy petting will come
back to you. Don't question these. They, too, are presents
you can keep so long as you open them alone and don't
use them in some silly poem. Girls' freckles and moles on trout,
like periods dotted by hand in sentences too sexy to say—
yes, Lord. Thank you for the small muscle a middling man
like me has. Give me wisdom, God, when I'm forty.
For now, come kiss me like a man friend. Make me born again.

Lent

Some, come Lent, give up things unknowingly—
daffodils, for one. Each March the low lemon trumpets
blow their color out of the clammy ground,
dotting the bounds of houses gone now,
each bloom an ember of memory honoring
the shapes of fallen shacks. Every year
this yellow surprises me, returning in plenty, precious,
saying they're not the first and you're not the first,
glad and quiet, drawing up from dirt the old salts,
the black goodness of the gone. Making petals of it.

Ash Monday

In their making mating we go gold, our pickups
  and porch swings dusted with the dry saffron
    of cypresses, gums, and sycamores in their, yes,
desire, in their upright, soaring sowing.
  Every body above ground is on loblolly's dance card, is
    to be powdered from on high with a sift of light-lipped,
breezy sugars. We are all of us heavy-petted by pine trees.
  Is the eighty-year oak easy or are we, accepting the seeds of seeds?
    And why does it feel like chastity? It can't be—
all Lent long being had by the waked-up hardwoods.
  There's no choosing. It's in the air. You can't refuse.
    The land of the living, coated with loving—Lord, lord.
  Let them come. Let them come.

Sweep

How sweet to move across this level floor
driving dropped crumbs before you
with a simple, ancient tool.
Broom up a mound of our kitchen's dust:
its sugars and salts, cornmeal, coffee,
snowy leavenings, poundcake crust.
Through a ginger scrim of onion skin,
divine the lost spectacle screw, the peridot
that plinked from its sterling post
by their peppercorn rattle, their shine
in the pile. None of it you knew you
dropped, which is why you sweep slow—
so eyes see, ears hear. The bristles' whisper
assembles and atones. Pan the grey pile,
then sow it outside. Call it one small
mountain moved. Planks, tiles, or vinyl
cobble of stones clean, kitchen ready
as turned loam (no field or kitchen
keeps this way for long), you feel
like a wind that has rinsed a plain.
The ground of our being is cleared.

Stranger

All along the stranger was there,
for years—still, between, watching
from cracks and corners, listening
from under our floor, party to
the children's first steps, to our muffled
loving, to the wrapping then ripping of gilt
papers, the dropped dishes and shoved
furniture, the hours of television
and piano practice and tears over math,
the inhabited silences. A presence
under our presence, in the margins.
An extra liver within our lives.
We should have heard the breathing
or the lack of breath. We should
have felt the other awake—
if not while we read cards and
tapped our pieces around the
board (for who hears then,
at play, that the outside can
come in as through a cellar door)—
if not together, then when some one
of us was alone, laying carpet or cleaning
or working at home. I should have heard
his silence. To be heard was why he had come.

Hands

We demand that hands remember the chord,
the half-hitch, how to dig postholes after years
of holding pencils, the planting of the long-fallow acres

once they are fenced—the parting of loam and roots,
the drizzle of seed. Also the gathering of wild blackberries
and the snaring of birds among the reaped canes.

Freeing a caught redwing calls for tender muscle,
a grip that holds without crushing, that weighs the give
of down and hollow bones, that thumbs softly

the strobing berry of the heart. Touch must see and hear.
Only one skilled in yielding can hold such a breakable
body and not hurt it—not hush what sings through

the frail, feather-light lacework of bird.
The skill of our hands scares us so, when we sleep
we send our hands away—do in our dreams without them.

They don't care. They are still there, married to their opposite
(who else?) and bearing it. *Just try to let us go*, they say. *Try.*
We have them and they hold us. They remember. They never cry.

Wish

Let me be this car thief with his slim jim,
slipping it in along the glass, deft flick
of wrist that clicks open the way elsewhere.
He takes what he needs not from meanness
or greed. He's just alive in the present,
like the first crack of a seed—a crevice
from which coiled desire will reach.
His next quick tool in this sequence is
silver metal paste pressed into the ignition
with firm gloved forefinger, using force
enough to lightly touch it to the tumblers.
Precisely as it cures he twists the sham key,
savoring the friction. The V8 roars. He's free.

Losers Weepers

This one wore a shirt so long a hard rain ripped the arms
off him. The seams tore with the weight of the water
and still he couldn't trash the threads.

Three wild birds this one has held: a towhee brained
by a window pane, a green-glittered thumb of a hummer,
a snow-numbed wren he warmed in his hoodie.
Two died in his hand. The hummer zithered south.

In high school, cheerleaders asked this one
for boy advice as he lettered their run-ins.
They said he was nice. The pawprints he painted
on their panties flashed when they flipped.

Each one sad, each wanting to be seen, if only
in a quick flicker, sequin-green. The boy, as small,
as weightless as the bird, watches the girls cheer
when their team tears through his words.

Boy Marries Girl

The preacher neither of them knows
flags a truck groaning up the mountain
and calls the driver to be their witness.
In the cinderblock church, the altar
is a sycamore driftlog slab, edges
still white-barked, the grain a truer
blonde than the bride. Inside her,
a butterbean of a baby, not this boy's,
nestles, tight as a bud. She likes how
the altar lets her see into a tree.
The groom wants to hand-plane
a kitchen table from such planks.
The preacher in his short sleeves
loans the young man his narrow tie
without un-noosing it. He lights
two candles, a Bible broken between
them, floating on the slab as the slab
floated in its eddy, things waiting
to be found. *This is holy ground,*
the minister lows. The trucker uncaps,
as in a diner, muses that there are
surprises wherever he goes.
His daughter died a decade ago
and the flow of the road has been
his comfort. The ring he has been
given (worn silver at its edges) is
a zero. At the right time in the vows
and motions they all know, he offers it.
Boy and girl kiss. Then they all go.

Funeral Home

You have a thread, he says, and plucks it from her shoulder,
his tug unstitching her blouse pocket and freeing a creased picture
which drifts to the quiet carpet: her and the dead girl.

I am so sorry, he says, stooping for the photo-booth square
of their kiss, overexposed. She goes for it, too, so they are close,
in a sudden frozen bow together. He sees down her shirt and rues

how he seems to be stealing things he doesn't mean to.
His ears burn. *It's ok,* she murmurs. Her eyes unglaze.
She lets him lift the picture from the hushed floor.

Did you kiss her, too? She asks. He tried *She was, like—No way!*
They almost laugh. *She let me. Only that one day.*
As they unbend, she tugs the thread from the last inch

of seam. *I'm all mine. That's what she used to say.*
She looks at the picture held out to her, remembers
the curtain on the booth had smelled like old shoes.

Nobody's getting kissed back now, she says. He sighs. *True.*
She hands him her pocket. *Here. Keep the picture, too.*

Tourist

Ahead of me to check in for the flight to Phoenix
is a boy in his thirties, tall, whose name
the ticket agent says out loud. *Not the Carney*
Collins who hit for the cycle in Asheville in '08?
Yes: that very one. *Oh my God! That game*, she says.
Mr. Collins, you were *that game.* She tells
all in earshot of the leadoff homer—first pitch,
first run. His head sinks one notch. After she
reels off the double in the fourth, then the backspin
bounce that got him to third under the tag, he stands
a full foot shorter. She fails to see his pilled sweatpants
and tired sneakers, the weight around his middle.
Who can blame her? Her love is not for him,
but for the elliptical luck of baseball, which brought
her in the company of her father to the misery
of a nine-run Tourist loss redeemed by one player's
minor ten-base miracle. Some look at a ruin and see
the city that was. I can't hear his reply. The fraying seams
and broken wheel on his suitcase fill my eye. I hear her
kiss his cheek. *Screw the majors. What a great try.*

Forty Leaven

Fortyleven

When my mother said it,
my sisters and I knew our needs
had pushed her to a brink (*Pulled*
fortyleven different ways at once..!)
where duties and deadlines drowned
her ability to think. I heard it wearing
my muddy cleats on the road to Ree's
piano lesson, heard it each canning
season from her clean kitchen, when
the church bulletin was half-typed
on the table in the steel Royal too heavy
by half a ton for me to lift, so her pickling
depended on my father's trucking his muscles
home from the garden. (He never did before dark.)
The fused numbers to a Mecklenburg girl
added up to a countrified infinity. Fortyleven
didn't weigh the fifty-first pound of mud
pressed into the five-pound bag. It named
the split seam and the mess—the rip
where order quit keeping. Forty marked
an edge too far: my father's leg, cracked
by a line-driven softball he'd just pitched,
hurt like forty. Little-girl-mama's toddler sister
somehow clumb up the barn loft ladder, my mother
had run like forty to the house for help.
Forty days and forty nights of rain on Noah said
one more drop, daylight or dark, would have
sunk the ark. Imagine eleven notches worse—
so dire a deluge no soul could come through—
a slew of labors, of slings and arrows giving her
too much to prove. I'm fortyleven now,
as my mother was then, as bruised by children's

trials and hungers, by failings often (some way)
my own, by love of my neighbor as I loathe myself,
and by my need to fill need. I hear her when I skin
my limit—how she spoke her irk and worry
into a mother's angry spell that held off both.
I see her on her porch swing with her coffee,
listing her greats and grands, Hallowe'en coming.
What will the young ones want to be? She sips. Sways.
Then, Christmas. Fortyleven presents to find, and a tree.

The Love of Christ Detail Shop

Sure, it's a lure: a way of opening wallets
and purses in this river town filled with churches.
But it is beautiful, this low, brick shop
painted purple, the corner windows tinted
but transparent, smoky as incense.
The apron with its siliconed cracks is wet
and dimly reflects the briery circle on the sign.
This dawn its dark bay, door rolled open,
stands empty except for shade and humble things,
put away with care: used tires stacked straight,
clear spray jugs brimmed blue, green, and gold
on their wheeled cart. There is a still rack of bleached
cloths folded and white in the early sun.
Nobody is here—and he loves us, every one.

Knees

These are my own: these leg hinges
that ache for days after I beat out a throw
from third to first in softball. They bend
just one way—lower me to loosen lug nuts
on my pickup, to pick up pecans, light a fire.
Their skin as thin over bone as hide
on a yupik kayak. They get me there.
One aches in rain, the other creaks on stairs,
nothing like the knees of cypress trees—
scaley knobs that grow from a fixed bend, a buttress,
a blunt canine that rises above where a root grips down.
No bud, leaf, or branch, broken-barked, worn as strong
and simple as bone from weathering the river—
the tree book says cypress knees breathe.
Snorkle, finger, tower, tooth—no word works to name
roots that point up as they drill down. After years of kneeling,
they come to encircle their trunk like a sunken crown.
These knees reach down to real ground.

My weak knees that bend just one way lower me to pray
except when there's rain. They pop and pine when they
pry me back up. A church sign says *Kneel down to rise.*
Words can't name the needs or beat out the throw. I still try.
I watch the cypress live on their knees mid-river. Tall.
Year after year, without sound. I watch them not drown.

Oil

On your head this morning—it is always morning
where you've come to now—the bright oil of birdsong
says *grateful, grateful*, says *come be little*
in these high temples the trees, come fill
your hollow bones with dawn and visions.

In this beginning there is a call so real it wets your hair.
Your white shirt soaks and clings to you. You are born.
What has made finch and snake and wren, what has wrought
light and the moon and every rapid on every river,
what has made words and given them to us
as dense and old and admirable as rocks,
what spun the zero void into somethingness—tea olive
and tanager, honey possum and larch, the turtle its own home,
burning tiger and brook trout and every baby,
mildew and sumac and salt, snow and dirt—
the *I am* that all is has said *You sing, too.*

Blackberries

Even single they are plural: every gun-blue BB
in each clustered one, blown green to red to
ink-black from a white bloom, is a period ending
a sentence of May days too sweet to say.
God, what a purple-red predicate, the sun its big, silent
subject, honing ruddy edges on the canes,
brewing jet blood in the many miniberries
amid the briers. They pop, a few, as you pluck
them or as they plunk into your coffee can.
Love your own minimal bloodshed in this harvest,
the thorn-tear and the chiggers that will burrow
your crotch as you steal breakfast from the birds.
Kiss the snake. Risk is the best butter for cobbler ever.

Bridge Swallow

Matthew 6:26

The mud nests that edge the eave of the bridge
  seem simple until I watch a male, his mouth a split seed,
ferry clay from upstream for a whole morning.
  He daubs it under the roadbed beak-full by beak-full,
building without hands a perfect bowl. By noon,
  he has begun to narrow it into a half-bottle.
He can spare four quick flits to pluck gnats from the air.
  To drink, he folds his wings, skims a sip of river,
then flares back into flight, skipping me like a flat chip
  of feldspar off the current's glinting warble.
Birds do sow. Birds reap. He eats, drinks, and sings for birth.
  His mate settles, chepping. He spackles her in with earth.

Sunset

I am 50 and fishing a September sunset at 14.
Here and there, circles appear on the pond's surface,
single ripples that ring outward from a center with no sound.
They have no cause I can see. The boy me casts faster, thinking
of bream under the mirror, kissing the underskin of their sky
as they do his freckles when he floats. He dreads the day's end,
drops and drops the spinner into these zeros to hook a life
and pull it out of the last daylight. These many years later,
I come still on that water. I stop casting to receive the circle's
silent spread. Watch its widening center wrinkle the first four
stars. I receive the pond, center of the pasture, pasture center
of the fenced-off field a stranger owns. Eye that never closes,
I see you now. I am not shut yet, life under, life over. I am
my own son and brother. You pull us to you like a lover.

Wasatchie Tanaga

Bruised by my climb down boulders and snow,
I let brook trout catch me all sunset.
I bow to three keepers. They don't blink.

Downwind of camp, so bears won't supper
on my muscle as I will on trout's,
my knife under the gill kills quickly—

opens each brother on the fir log
scrapes his rosy organs onto wood: gut
that gave him up to my gut. I keep

this shared pink cup of hunger whole. I
return it to the creek. Dipped tin mug
washes the blade, the bloody altar,

my cracked hands. The grey slab, rinsed, flares bright
as our fire. Stone, stream, fish, coals—one smoke
rises, weaving, shoaling the stars. Whole.

Area 51: Birthday Eve

Exit your age by way of Oregon, Georgia boy,
by way of first footsink into Pacific sand
first fragrance of Douglass fir, first earful
of frog-creak, first eyefall up to Cascades snow.
  Growing up Baptist, no hand wet
your baby head, so it's high time to be
misted like a Sitka spruce by holy Wahkeena
and Horsetail, to be christened wild, withheld
from hell by a secondhand soaking from plasma
torch cataracts creasing old, cold lava as they have
for the last sixty centuries. Touch your boot toes
to the cold lap in the basalt bowl, black salver
catching white gout, cup running over.
The Falls' birthday sermon—*It's early in eternity*—
deafens you. Stand here in the flow and you might
wear down to your real root, like the python
gripping that Ponderosa pine into the rock slope.
Play off your groping as grasp. Act like you're
sure and secure as a padlock clicked shut in a hasp.
Or glory solo, show your ass, for there's not one
witness out here with you: 51 is restricted access.
So learn what will fly. Genuflect to saucers fallen
from the sky, to the alien you inside. Godspeed,
test pilot. Grip the dawn stick of X-52. Morning is nigh.

After Kelcey Freezes My Pre-Cancer

my ear cools and I come down from the adrenal shot
of the aerosol cold, my whole body awed by the subarctic burn
in this one member, my skin aware that an edge of it
has been made to die—has already begun to blister. Each evening
a rust flake will crack, then shed from the ridge of cartilage
that has drunk too much sun funneling sound into me.
Each flake is a map written in my skin of where I have been,
where the trail has blazed me. I lose one Sapphic onion-paper
scrap, one milli-page, each day. First to go is the afterglow
of the Suwannee. Then the Okefenokee, where I burned in winter,
then Big Sneak rapid left of Forty Acre Island—there, light
sniped through canopy. Night by night under the bathroom bulb
I will knap another red mica sliver of self, facet and scab
of mortality fired over forty summers in the welling solar kiln
of creation. He who has ear to hear, let him hear.
In the cool of the evening I read the leaves of me,
see again what the body is:
more and less myself.

Two-Hand Touch

Two steps from the sideline, my seventeen-year-old son cuts
up-field so that my lunge to touch-tackle him turns mid-air
to a slow-motion dive past the grass toward the cement sidewalk
edging it. I descend as if this second had seventy increments,
every one as distinct and ball-peened by disaster as the shards
of a crashed, dredged, re-pieced Boeing. Frame by frame
I both watch and film my fall. My boy's quick pivot is not
in the picture, but my heart so crows his grace that his juke
is the bright bulb behind the whole reel, limning each sand grain,
each carat of quartz on the concrete plain I'm on final approach to.
My pink palms chock down like landing gear, blinking chinks of green
glass catching light between them in the eon preceding the skid
of my hand-heel's skin against pavement and my yaw and roll
onto elbow, knee, and shoulder. My outer self will shred,
white cheddar on a grater. Some socketed bone will unseat,
my hide constellate with red dwarf suns of blood. I can't
see my boy for the ground but I know, in my long father's fall,
he runs on. Every wound my body blooms will shout *Go! Go!*

At the Counter, Len Berg's

The man on the stool next to me orders beef tips, peas, and rice.
The waitress waits. *What else do I want?* He asks. *Do you know?*
Some questions asked right are answers, hot as cornbread.
What I want: to sit in the ink-blue oceans children paint,
to daily pray in the pitch and catch of curve balls, to tell
the waitress in words she would trust how pretty
it is that she has brought me fried corn, apples, and okra
six minutes after I sat down. To go to the fair at two
on a Thursday and be rolled up to to a swinging stop
way high on the ferris wheel in a sunny sprinkle
of rain, then be circled down and asked to judge
the home-canned bread and butter pickles.
I wallow in wishes, waiting for him to turn
and include me in his question. I will be wise,
maybe, this once. Then the pretty waitress
squints one eye and says, absolutely right: *Pie.*

Eyes

Eyes, you used to seize every edge—
each stitch on a breaking baseball,

the inky undulation of Sister Sledge
as the LP grooved us back to the animal.

You tightroped the seams of cocktail dresses,
fell from the upended horizons of their hems.

The least ripple of a bedding bluegill's fin
across lit creek-bottom zeroed you in.

You were happy, Lefty, to shut as your bro
notched a Coors can's *o* then put a bullet through it—

but now, leaf blurs into bough, the sunflower petal
and the lamp flame into the same yolk-stroke

of Van Gogh. Reading is like tracking mice on snow.
So I'm writing it big: you're benched, twin bros.

Fingers, skin, you're in. Feel it all. Fill us. Know.

Crossing Mukilteo Ferry

Wired and gritty-eyed after a wakeful night
worrying that we would miss it, I stand
at the stern at dawn and watch as Whidbey
recedes over the white fizz of wake.
My family sleeps in the car, the last to drive on.
To escape the cold, I take the stairs to the cabin,
walking toward the bow between rows of empty seats.
A woman, sixties, prays her rosary in t shirt and jeans.
A paunchy teen speedwalks laps, earbuds in.
An old man, eyes closed, his head in a woman's
ample lap, his cap still on, dozes. Here and there,
six heads bend over books: these readers seem
like a constellation of distant cousins.
Behind the commissary counter, three women in hair nets
chat as one makes change for coffee to a girl in gauges
and a man's Carhart coat.

In an empty portside booth, the pieced edges of a puzzle
frame in blue and green the white tabletop—a visible silence
waiting to be filled, crossing by crossing, by whoever cares
to share in the work. How many different fingers will sort
and piece the colors, no box or photo to go by? I fret
that no one will sit down and fit the picture any further
together. In groups, at sustained patience, among folks going
on faith to figure things out, I don't count, so I go out on deck.

In wind, Clinton comes on, the coast craggy, all juts and nooks.
The variegation of the car deck, where each sedan and coupe
is a small, different-colored country, feels like a flat, jigsaw map.
Two Harleys kneel at the rail. Through a gap in the gray caul
of sky, miles down the way, a ray of sun pours like light
through an attic door, to make one far acre of sea-wobble glitter.

I picture the faces of my family sleeping on, under glass.
(Am I their dream? They would laugh. They would like that.)
I want to keep the sight—my girl and boys, my wife, at rest in
a car on a boat—each face a bead strung, a piece in its place.

One way to pray is to think *Thank you* and mean it, despite
the cracks in the whole. At the Clinton dock, the channel light
has stayed lit. We thrum toward it. At the bow, a dozen of
the co-carried form a ferry-prow congregation as we close in.
We feel in our soles the diesels go dumb, the ark slowing.
The man in the cap holds the ample woman's hand.
Every patient face is awake to the one place we are all going.

Heart

1. Auricle

Spiders, I have read, walk with their hearts,
which pump blood like brake fluid
into the tricky, articulate joints of their legs.
Twenty years ago I wrote it down. This dawn
as I shave, that cardiac fact leads me for the third day
to take care not to wash the seed-sized weaver
with my whiskers down the drain. I tear two
squares of tissue and lay their corner before him
to climb onto so I can carry him on this magic
carpet outside, not looking into a single one
of his four pairs of eyes—only letting
his horned quark of a heart, unheard,
beat his eight fingering legs into the yard.

2. Ventricle

All day after, my knees systole-diastole me
where I have to go—the kitchen for coffee,
three miles of run, goosing the Tacoma to work,
then bearing me back out to it in the setting sun.
Familiar loop of my only day, circular as the sink
too round, steep, and slick for the spider to crest.
The mote of him toeing up in a widening spiral,
untiring, until his grip on the vitreous gave
and he slipped, was boulder, Sisyphus, me.
The instant his fifth foot found an iota of friction
to stop the slide, all seven others tickled into stride.
His eight. My two. My hips and ankles, my jog-sore
thighs. Our hearts like bloody bagpipes blow.
I palm mine: *try, try. Try, try. Try.*

Scaring the Bears

Over the edge in the fog
that has risen from the river
below, his boots on the switch-
back path descend. Every seventh
step he speaks. *Hey there*, he says.
Morrel! Stephanie Atkinson! Foley grip!
He says *Manifest destiny* and *Not munificent.*
In places the way is scree: his soles sliding stones
make noise enough. In the laurel hells he gets louder:
Now how much would you pay? Finnegan's fake!
He feels more and less alone. *Another mother*
further. Meaning doesn't matter.
It's just sound to save his life
until after he has fished.

White Shirt

Thank you God for this page I don't have to fill with words,
for the joy of being blank, finding in the closet a silence
I can wear. Reaching fingers through these sleeves of snow
I can love the plain of me, covered, become a glass of cold milk.
I will let this placket of flat pearls hold me shut, and shut I will fill,
full as a sail, my one pocket empty, waiting for what gets found.
Cuffs closed, neck open, a bandage showing no blood, I will not
mean but be, drawing daylight like a clean kitchen curtain,
certain that a man, like this, can be a bride.

The Author

Gordon Johnston has written two chapbooks, *Durable Goods* (Finishing Line Press) and *Gravity's Light Grip* (Perkolator Press), co-authored with Matthew Jennings *Ocmulgee National Monument: A Brief Guide with Field Notes*, and published poems and prose in *The Georgia Review*, *Southern Poetry Review*, and other journals. He also writes clay pages—poems wood-fired into stoneware by Roger Jamison. Director of the Georgia Poetry Circuit from 1996–2007, Johnston is professor of English at Mercer University, where he directed Creative Writing until 2017.